D0579259

I Am Honest

By Mark Erroll

Gareth Stevens
Publishing

Please visit our Web site, www.garethstevens.com. For a free color catalog of all our high-quality books, call toll free 1-800-542-2595 or fax 1-877-542-2596.

Library of Congress Cataloging-in-Publication Data

Erroll, Mark.
  I am honest / Mark Erroll.
     p. cm. — (Kids of character)
  Includes index.
  ISBN 978-1-4339-4863-3 (pbk.)
  ISBN 978-1-4339-4864-0 (6-pack)
  ISBN 978-1-4339-4862-6 (library binding)
  1. Honesty–Juvenile literature. 2. Children–Conduct of life–Juvenile literature. I. Title.
  BJ1533.H7E77 2011
  179'.9–dc22

                                    2010034640

First Edition

Published in 2011 by
Gareth Stevens Publishing
111 East 14th Street, Suite 349
New York, NY 10003

Editor: Mary Ann Hoffman
Designer: Christopher Logan

Photo credits: Cover, pp. 1, 5, 7, 11, 17, 19 Shutterstock.com; p. 9 Banana Stock/Thinkstock; pp. 13, 21 iStockphoto.com; p. 15 Hemera/AbleStock.com/Thinkstock.

Printed in the United States of America

CPSIA compliance information: Batch #CW11GS: For further information contact Gareth Stevens, New York, New York at 1-800-542-2595.

Table of Contents

Boldface words appear in the glossary.

Being Honest

An honest person tells the truth. They do their own work. An honest person is fair to others. They take care of things that belong to others. An honest person can be trusted.

In the Neighborhood

Ron found money on the sidewalk.
He told his mother about the money.
It belonged to their neighbor. Ron
gave the money to their neighbor.
Ron is honest.

Dena was playing ball with her friends. She hit the ball. The ball broke the neighbor's window. Dena told the neighbor the truth. Dena is honest.

At School

Ava's teacher asked to see her homework. Ava had not done it. She had played outside instead. She told her teacher why she did not have her homework. Ava is honest.

The children were taking a test. Ed did his own work. He did not **copy** other people's answers. Ed is honest.

A school rule says you must walk, not run, down the stairs. Jake was alone on the stairs. No one would see if he ran. But Jake walked down the stairs. Jake is honest.

At Home

Mom asked Cara to clean her room. Cara talked on the phone instead. Mom asked her if her room was clean. Cara said, "No." She told the truth. Cara is honest.

Peter wanted to ride his brother's bike. He asked his brother if he could ride it. He did not just take it. Peter is honest.

Greg had a book from the **library**. It got wet when he put it on the grass. Greg took the book back to the library. He told them the truth. Greg is honest.

Glossary

copy: to use someone else's work as your own

library: a place to get books to read

For More Information

Books

Nettleton, Pamela Hill. *Is That True? Kids Talk About Honesty.* Minneapolis, MN: Picture Window Books, 2005.

Thomas, Pat. *I'm Telling the Truth: A First Look at Honesty.* Hauppauge, NY: Barron's Educational Series, 2006.

Web Sites

Honesty
www.k12.hi.us/ ~mkunimit/honesty.htm
Learn what it means to be honest. Read examples of how an honest person acts.

Honesty
www.intime.uni.edu/citizenship/themes/single_themes/honesty.htm
Read examples of honest behaviors.

Index